Eat Your U.S. History
HOMEWORK

Recipes for Revolutionary Minds

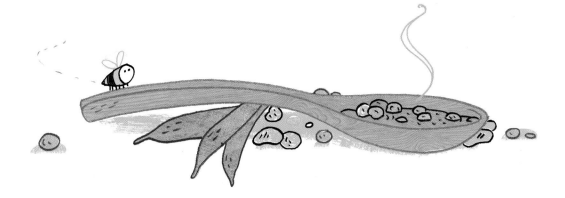

Ann McCallum

Illustrated by Leeza Hernandez

ini Charlesbridge

To Aliya and Kamran—north of the border.
—A. M.

Historical hugs of gratitude to Ann, Julie, and
Martha—thank you!
—L. H.

Table of Contents

Introduction

Ah-choo! Oh, no, a sneezing attack! It happens every time you open your dusty, old history textbook. That is, if you stay awake long enough to sneezzzzzz. . . . But wait, history doesn't need to be deadly dull. In fact, it is anything but boring when you munch and crunch your way through it. Get set for a guaranteed way to turn sneezy into easy and drowsy into delicious. Get ready to eat your history homework!

This is a book about making edible connections to American history. Each section shares a quick bite of America from 1620 to 1789, highlighting events—and food—from the arrival of the Pilgrims to George Washington becoming the first president. The recipes are based on original descriptions or on what historians believe early colonists were eating at the time. Of course, before Europeans settled in what we now call North America, the "new" world was old news to millions of Native Americans who had called this land home for thousands of years. As cultures collided, people learned to survive by sharing ideas—and food.

Any way you slice it, learning about the past has never been so tasty!

Note: Words in **bold** can be found in the glossary on page 44.

1607: The first permanent English colony is founded at Jamestown, Virginia.

1619: The first African slaves are brought to Jamestown, Virginia.

1620: Pilgrims sail from England to settle in America.

1622: European honeybees are brought to America.

1641: Slavery is legalized in Massachusetts, and other colonies follow.

1650: Tea is imported to New Amsterdam. (That's New York City to us.)

1732: Georgia, the last of the thirteen original colonies, is founded.

1754: The French and Indian War, also known as the Seven Years' War, begins.

1763: The Treaty of Paris officially ends the French and Indian War.

1765: The Stamp Act requires colonists to pay taxes on printed goods.

1773: The Boston Tea Party is held to protest British taxes.

1775: The American Revolutionary War begins.

1776: America signs the Declaration of Independence.

1783: The Treaty of Paris (another treaty by this name!) officially ends the American Revolutionary War.

1784: George Washington buys a cream machine for ice.

1789: George Washington is elected as the first U.S. president.

Kitchen Tips

Cooking your way through history can be a risky business if you are not careful. Please ask an adult to assist you, especially when things are sharp or hot.

Tricks of the Trade

- Read everything before you begin, and make sure you understand the directions.
- Wash your hands thoroughly.
- Gather everything you will need ahead of time (some ingredients like margarine or butter are easier to work with when they are at room temperature).
- Give yourself enough space to work.

One more thing—these recipes have been modernized to fit our current lifestyles. (Um, did you really want to use bear grease instead of a stick of butter? Or skin a squirrel for that casserole?)

Thanksgiving Succotash

*C*an you please pass the venison, *pumpion*, and wild fowl? (That is, the deer meat, stewed pumpkin, and wild turkeys and ducks—yum!) These foods may not be your typical holiday fare today, but at the celebration that became known as the first Thanksgiving, these were some of the dishes that may have been gobbled up.

In September 1620, a group of 102 **Pilgrims** left Europe. They were headed for Virginia, though bad weather forced them to land farther north. The Pilgrims wanted to settle in North America because they were not allowed to practice their religion the way they wanted to in Europe. Plus, European cities were overcrowded (and stinky), and there weren't enough jobs.

These Pilgrims sailed for sixty-five days in a cramped ship called the ***Mayflower***, eating mostly dried meat and fish and hardened crackers. Finally reaching land, the Pilgrims met the Wampanoag—an **indigenous people** who had been living in America for thousands of years.

In the Pilgrims' new home, **Plymouth** (which is part of Massachusetts today), the food ran out, and many got sick. Almost half of the Pilgrims died during that first winter. In fact, if the Wampanoag people hadn't stepped in to help, they may not have made it at all.

With the Wampanoag teaching the Pilgrims how to hunt and grow food, there was suddenly plenty to eat. To celebrate, the Pilgrims invited more than ninety of these Native Americans to join in a three-day feast. We don't know exactly what they served, but likely a version of succotash was part of the menu. Also, they didn't call this celebration "Thanksgiving," but the Pilgrims were more than thankful to have survived that first year.

Pass the peas and corn, please! Making this modernized succotash is easy-*peasy*.

Thanksgiving Succotash • • • • • • • • • • •

BEFORE YOU BEGIN

Prep time: 15 minutes
Cooking time: 10 minutes
Total time: 25 minutes

Oven temperature: n/a
Yield: 4 servings
Difficulty: medium

EQUIPMENT

12-inch nonstick frying pan
Large, sturdy spoon
Table knife and cutting board
Serving bowl

INGREDIENTS

- 4 slices bacon (turkey or pork)
- 1 cup frozen sweet corn
- ½ cup frozen peas
- ½ cup frozen lima beans
- 2 hot dogs, cut into half-inch pieces
- ½ cup chicken stock
- Pepper and salt to taste

METHOD

1 Place bacon in frying pan and cook until it starts to get crisp.

2 Remove and cut into bite-size pieces using the table knife and cutting board.

3 Put frozen corn, peas, lima beans, cut-up bacon, hot dog pieces, and seasonings in the same pan.

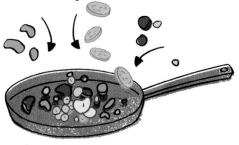

4 Add the chicken stock. Stir frequently, until the veggies are cooked.

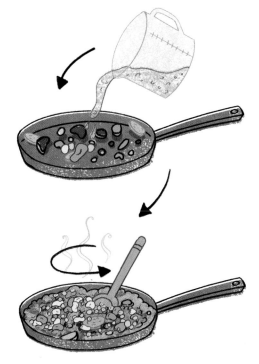

5 Place in serving bowl and enjoy!

9

Thanksgiving Succotash • • •

Officially a Feast!

The Pilgrims didn't celebrate with a Thanksgiving feast every year. However, over time and throughout the colonies, various groups did observe special days of thanks. In the mid-1800s Sarah Josepha Hale (author of the poem "Mary Had a Little Lamb") argued that Thanksgiving should be a national holiday. Finally, in 1863, President Abraham Lincoln proclaimed that the last Thursday in November would be the official Thanksgiving. Then, in 1941, President Franklin D. Roosevelt signed a bill into law stating that the national holiday would always be the fourth Thursday in November. Thank goodness for Thanksgiving!

SIDE DISH

Thanks to one Native American in particular, a man named Squanto, the Pilgrims learned how to gather and grow food from what was available. He showed them how to cultivate corn by placing a seed in the ground along with a dead fish to fertilize the soil. (*Pee-ew!* But, hey, it worked.) Squanto also taught them which berries to eat and how to hunt wild turkeys by calling to them with a homemade whistle.

Food in America was much different from what the Pilgrims were used to back in Europe.

Take a look inside your refrigerator. Which food items would not have been available to the Pilgrims in the 1600s?

Colonial Cherry-Berry Grunt

*E*eeergh! There was a lot of grunting and groaning in the early days of America's **thirteen original colonies**. Learning to survive and thrive in this new land wasn't a piece of cake. After the Pilgrims settled in America, **colonists** from countries such as France, Spain, the Netherlands, and others sailed to America. Some people came to get rich quick—they searched for gold or traded for fur with the Native Americans. Others settled in permanently. Everyone who arrived in America needed food and shelter. Some colonists first lived in crude dugouts—wood-lined holes with a tree bark roof (*Ahem*—spider alert!)—until they could build more comfortable cabins.

Forget microwaves. Forget electric or gas stoves and ovens. Instead colonists hung pots from hooks in a large, open fireplace and let things simmer. They baked bread in covered pans placed on the warm stone hearth. In the warmer months, wild berries, grapes, and crabapples were available. The colonists had to learn to embrace strange, new ingredients such as deer meat and corn. They missed foods from their various native countries. Then, as ship after ship came, new settlers brought seeds for wheat, apples, cherries, and other familiar foods. Life got a little sweeter when someone thought to import honeybees in 1622. America became a blend of old and new—and we're not just talking about dinner!

Traditionally called a grunt or slump, nowadays this next treat is referred to as a cobbler. Its original name comes from the sound of the fruit as it bubbles on the stove—that is, in the moments before you eat it!

Colonial Cherry-Berry Grunt • • • • • • • • •

BEFORE YOU BEGIN

Prep time: 15 minutes
Cooking time: 25 minutes +
   10 minutes to set
Total time: 55 minutes

Oven temperature: n/a
Yield: 4–6 servings
Difficulty: medium

INGREDIENTS

- ½ cup sugar
- ¼ cup butter
- 1 egg
- 1 teaspoon vanilla
- ¾ cup flour
- 1 teaspoon baking powder
- ¼ cup milk
- 20-ounce can cherry pie filling
- ¾ cup fresh or frozen berries
  (blueberries, blackberries, or raspberries)

EQUIPMENT

9 ½-inch sauté pan with lid (or other
   shallow pan with lid)
Large mixing bowl
Sturdy spoon or electric mixer

METHOD

1 Empty the can of cherry pie filling into sauté pan. Heat until warm and bubbling.

2 In a separate dish, make the topping. Beat together sugar and butter. Stir in the egg, vanilla, and milk. Add the flour and baking powder and mix just until combined.

3 Carefully combine the frozen berries and the topping.

4 Spoon the topping dough over the warm cherry pie filling. Cover the pan with a tight-fitting lid and continue cooking on the stovetop for 25 minutes, or until the topping is firm.

5 Turn off heat and allow to sit for 10 minutes before serving. (And since it's not the 1600s, serve with ice cream if you like!)

Colonial Cherry-Berry Grunt • • • • • • • • • •

Calling All Colonies!

By 1732, European settlers had established what became known as the thirteen original colonies. Do the names of these colonies ring a bell?

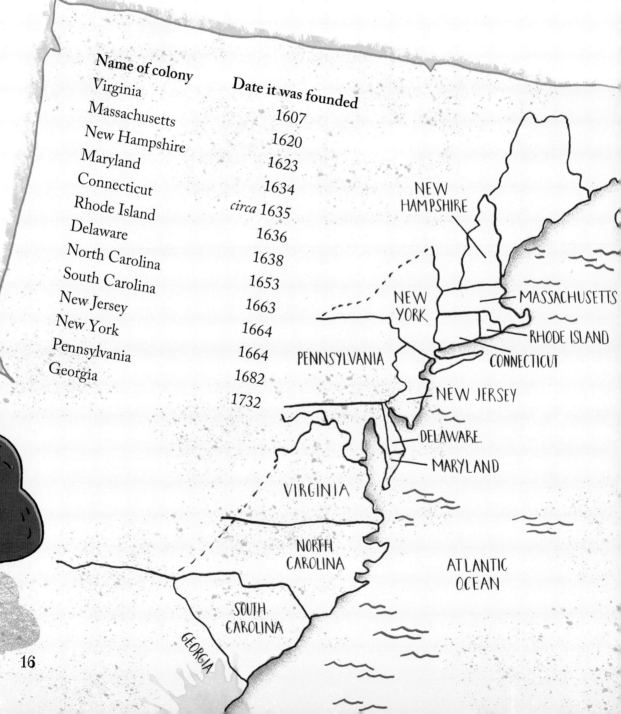

Name of colony	Date it was founded
Virginia	1607
Massachusetts	1620
New Hampshire	1623
Maryland	1634
Connecticut	circa 1635
Rhode Island	1636
Delaware	1638
North Carolina	1653
South Carolina	1663
New Jersey	1664
New York	1664
Pennsylvania	1682
Georgia	1732

NEW HAMPSHIRE

NEW YORK

MASSACHUSETTS

RHODE ISLAND

CONNECTICUT

PENNSYLVANIA

NEW JERSEY

DELAWARE

MARYLAND

VIRGINIA

NORTH CAROLINA

ATLANTIC OCEAN

SOUTH CAROLINA

GEORGIA

SIDE DISH

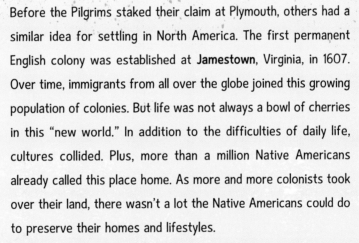

Before the Pilgrims staked their claim at Plymouth, others had a similar idea for settling in North America. The first permanent English colony was established at **Jamestown**, Virginia, in 1607. Over time, immigrants from all over the globe joined this growing population of colonies. But life was not always a bowl of cherries in this "new world." In addition to the difficulties of daily life, cultures collided. Plus, more than a million Native Americans already called this place home. As more and more colonists took over their land, there wasn't a lot the Native Americans could do to preserve their homes and lifestyles.

Can you imagine what kind of hardships both the Native Americans and the colonists faced? What would it be like to experience an influx of new people—with different ideas about civilization— to your homeland? What would it be like to move to a place with a new climate, new terrain, and without many of your friends and family from back home?

Lost Bread

By the middle of the 1700s, most colonists were farmers. Cities and towns had sprung up, and schools were established. Life in the colonies was a little more settled. Across the ocean, England and France each wanted to claim America for its own. Neither country considered that America belonged to its original inhabitants—the Native Americans. France wanted to continue its profitable **fur trade**, eventually controlling the whole continent. England also wanted control, so it could provide a place for English citizens to settle.

The fight was on! The **French and Indian War**, named after the French and their Native American allies, lasted from 1754 to 1763. The British wanted the French *out* of North America, so they sent Major George Washington to warn the French to leave. It didn't work. Next they sent General Braddock to root out the French from a critical stronghold: **Fort Duquesne** (pronounced Du-KANE).

As the British trekked through the wilderness, soldiers ate what they could hunt or gather, or food the army provided. This included corn meal, beans, goober peas (boiled peanuts), bacon, and **hardtack**. A twice-baked type of cracker, hardtack was so hard that soldiers had to be careful not to chip a tooth when eating it. If lucky, a soldier might get a piece of pork and a spoonful of brown sugar to put on top of it. Meanwhile, the French enjoyed tasty *pain perdu* (translated, this means "lost bread," also called French toast by the English). The treat was named for its main ingredient: stale bread that would otherwise be thrown away.

Eventually the **Treaty of Paris** was signed in 1763, and France lost this war. But the country will never lose its flair for the delicious!

Lost Bread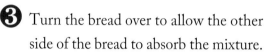

BEFORE YOU BEGIN

Prep time: 15 minutes
Cooking time: 2 minutes per slice
Total time: 23 minutes

Oven temperature: n/a
Yield: 4 slices (2 servings)
Difficulty: medium

INGREDIENTS

- Day-old bread, cut into 1-inch slices (challah or other firm bread works well)
- ⅔ cups milk
- 1 tablespoon brown sugar
- 2 eggs
- ½ teaspoon vanilla
- Butter
- Maple syrup

EQUIPMENT

Pie plate or other deep dish
Whisk or fork
Sturdy, nonstick skillet
Spatula

METHOD

 Whip eggs with a whisk or fork. Add milk, brown sugar, and vanilla, and pour into the pie plate.

❷ Place the bread slices in the egg mixture and allow to soak up liquid.

❸ Turn the bread over to allow the other side of the bread to absorb the mixture.

❹ Melt a little butter in a nonstick skillet. Place soaked bread slices in the hot skillet. Cook on each side until browned.

 Remove the bread using the spatula and serve immediately with maple syrup drizzled on top.

21

Lost Bread • • • •

Hungry to Attack

The British prepared for the key battle of the French and Indian War: the **Battle of Quebec**. On a high cliff with plenty of cannons and soldiers, the city of Quebec was tricky to attack. At first the British commander, General Wolfe, thought he would cut off supplies to the fort and wait until the people inside starved—everyone has to eat, right? Then he had a better (and faster) idea. On the night of September 13, 1759, the British got lucky. Sneaking up a narrow cliff path, 4,500 British soldiers assembled in a field outside the walls of Quebec. They attacked at dawn. In just a few minutes, the British had won. Given the terrain, this was a surprising feat. Soon it was *au revoir* to most of France's American colonies.

22

SIDE DISH

At one time called Fort Duquesne, this area of land—another important stronghold during the French and Indian War—went through more name changes than, well, times we've been told to eat our veggies.

Shannopin (a Native American
village) became . . .   → **Fort Prince George**

Fort Prince George
(a British fort) became . . .   → **Fort Duquesne**

Fort Duquesne (taken over by the French
and named after the governor of New France,
Marquis Duquesne) became . . .   → **Fort Pitt**

Fort Pitt (retaken by the British
and named after the prime minister
of England) became . . .   → **Pittsburgh**
                                           (the modern-day city that
                                           now rests on this site).

Where *do* the names of cities and other places come from?
Hmmm . . . how about New York, Virginia, Mississippi,
Boston, and your home town?

QUEBEC MAP

Southern Plantation Hoe Cakes

Can you imagine what it was like to be a slave in colonial America? Every day you were told when to get up, what to eat, and what work to do. You didn't get paid, and you didn't go to school. You might even be separated from your family forever. There was no reasonable way to protest. The punishment for a disobedient slave was to be whipped—or worse.

Initially, about twenty Africans were brought to Jamestown, Virginia, in 1619. They were kidnapped from their homes in Africa, shipped to America, and sold and treated like *things* instead of people. Over the next two hundred years, slave traders brought thousands of Africans to America. Many of these men, women, and children worked on southern **plantations**, huge farms that were more like mini-cities. Plantation slaves worked twelve to fifteen hours a day for their owner and still kept their own gardens to supplement the minimal food they were given. They might even have done a little hunting and fishing to add extra meat to their meals.

For lunch, "hoe cakes" could be cooked right beside the field. All you had to do was mix up some cornmeal and water and place it near a small fire using a hoe. At least that's one theory. Others say that a gardening hoe wasn't used at all—instead, this type of "hoe" referred to an iron pan that was used to prepare the pancake-like food.

We don't have slavery in America any more, thankfully. In 1865 the **13th amendment** to the United States Constitution made it illegal to own another person.

Nowadays, these tasty cakes—once a tradition on the plantations—remain a hearty dish for anyone and everyone.

Southern Plantation Hoe Cakes • • • • • • •

Before You Begin

Prep time: 10 minutes
Cooking time: 2 minutes per hoe cake
Total time: 30 minutes

Oven temperature: n/a
Yield: 10 hoe cakes
Difficulty: medium

Ingredients

- 1 cup cornmeal
- ¾ cup flour
- ¼ teaspoon salt
- 2 teaspoons baking powder
- 1 egg
- 1 ⅓ cups milk
- 3 tablespoons melted butter
- Nonstick cooking spray
- Optional: butter or jam for serving

Equipment

Nonstick skillet or griddle
Spatula
Large mixing bowl

Method

1 Heat a skillet or griddle and spray with nonstick cooking spray.

2 In a large mixing bowl, stir together the cornmeal, flour, salt, and baking powder.

3 In a separate bowl, combine the egg and milk, stirring briskly.

4 Form a hole in the middle of the dry ingredients. Pour in the melted butter and then egg mixture. Stir well, but do not beat.

5 With adult help, slowly pour about a quarter cup of batter onto the hot skillet or griddle. Repeat with more batter, but make sure that the hoe cakes are not touching.

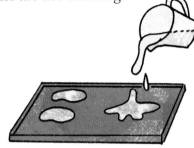

6 When slight bubbles form in the dough, turn each hoe cake over with the spatula. Cook the other side, about 30 seconds to a minute, or until browned.

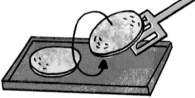

7 Remove from pan and serve warm, with butter or jam.

Southern Plantation Hoe Cakes • • • • • •

Thankful for the Gifts

"I know that supper will be big, Shuck that corn before you eat.
I think I smell a fine roast pig, Shuck that corn before you eat."

Sometimes several plantation owners would bring their slaves together to have a "corn-shucking festival." While shucking corn, African slaves often sang songs. Was this all music and fun? Not at all. The slaves had to work hard taking the husks off enormous mounds of corn, and the songs helped them to express their anguish.

Through their singing, African slaves introduced their music and language to America, including banjos, Congo dancing, and words like *okay*, *banana*, *tote*, and *bug*. It's also believed that they brought foods such as watermelon, black-eyed peas, and African rice with them to the New World.

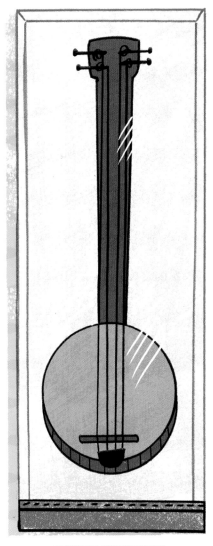

BANJO

CHAINS

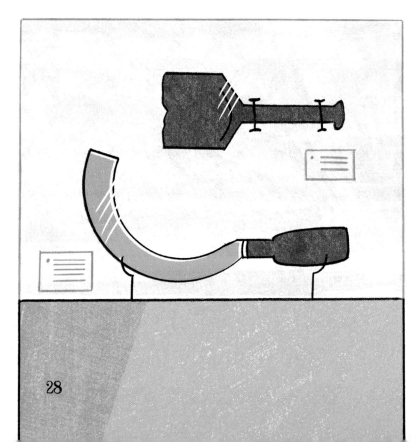

SIDE DISH

As the population of the colonies grew, America became an amazing "soup mixture" of different people from all over the globe. Among them were:

- The many tribes of Native Americans (pushed farther and farther west as Europeans forced them from their lands)
- The **frontier settlers** who lived away from populated areas and relied on hunting and farming to survive
- Merchants, craftspeople, **indentured servants**, and others who lived in cities. Indentured servants were Europeans who agreed to work for a certain period of time in exchange for the cost of passage to America.
- Small farmers who sold their surplus crops to the rest of the colonists
- Plantation owners who possessed town-sized areas of land and were often the wealthiest colonists
- Slaves—men, women, and children forced to leave their homes in Africa and come to America to work for free

How was life different for each of these groups? In what ways did all these different people interact?

TOOLS

EXIT

Revolutionary Honey-Jumble Cookies

Something was brewing in America in 1773, and it wasn't just coffee or tea. Anger towards the British parliament was about to boil over. On December 16, colonists organized a protest called the **Boston Tea Party**. They climbed aboard three ships and dumped forty-five tons of British-owned tea into the Boston Harbor. There was a new taste in the air: WAR.

England had spent a lot of money fighting against the French in America, and now—at least according to the British—it was payback time. Britain passed a law called the **Stamp Act**. Every time someone wanted to print something on paper—a newspaper, advertisement, or even playing cards—they had to pay a tax to Britain and get a stamp to prove it. Pretty soon colonists were crying out, **"Taxation without representation!"** No fair! Why should England tax the colonists when America had no say in the government of Britain?

England continued to tax the colonists. Things like lead, glass, paper, paint, and tea now cost a little extra. The colonists retaliated by **boycotting**, or refusing to buy British goods.

Parliament passed several laws that the colonists quickly named the **Intolerable Acts** because they didn't want to accept them. One of these laws closed the Boston Harbor. Another forced colonists to allow British soldiers to stay at their houses and eat their food. Bostonians could be forced to make dinner for uninvited—and unwanted—British "guests." *Grrr!* Anger flared on both sides of the ocean.

With no official colonial government, **patriots**—Americans against British rule—met in taverns and coffee houses to plan what to do next. On the menu was coffee and Honey-Jumble Cookies—with a dollop of politics, of course!

Revolutionary Honey-Jumble Cookies • • • • •

BEFORE YOU BEGIN

Prep time: 30 minutes
Cooking time: 8–12 minutes
Total time: 42 minutes

Oven temperature: 400° F
Yield: 30 cookies
Difficulty: medium

INGREDIENTS

- ¾ cup butter
- 1 ¼ cups sugar
- 2 eggs
- 1 tablespoon honey
- 2 ¾ cups flour
- 1 teaspoon baking powder
- ¼ teaspoon salt
- Topping: 1 teaspoon cinnamon,
  2 tablespoons sugar

EQUIPMENT

Large mixing bowl
Sturdy spoon or electric mixer
Cookie sheet
Shallow bowl
Smooth-bottomed glass
Spatula
Cookie racks

METHOD

1 Ask an adult to preheat the oven to 400° F.

2 Mix the butter and sugar together. Add the eggs and honey.

3 Blend together the flour, salt, and baking powder. Stir into the butter mixture.

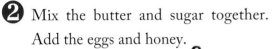

4 Chill dough in the fridge for at least 10 minutes to make it easier to handle.

5 Mix the cinnamon and 2 teaspoons of sugar. Place in a shallow bowl.

6 Form the dough into balls. Roll in the cinnamon mixture and then place on an ungreased cookie sheet, 2 inches apart. Slightly flatten each ball with the bottom of a glass or a spoon.

7 Bake for about 8–12 minutes (check to see that the cookies are slightly browned on the edges). When done, transfer to cookie racks to cool.

Revolutionary Honey-Jumble Cookies

That's the Way the Cookie Jumbles!

In America, we call them cookies. In England and other parts of the world, the same thing is called a biscuit. Maybe colonists got the name from the Dutch settlers who called these sweet treats *koekje*—sounds kind of like 'cookie', right? Sugar cookies and their variations have been around for a long time. German settlers from Pennsylvania called them Nazareth cookies. Later, someone had the crazy idea to call them *snickerdoodles*.

cookies

koekje

SIDE DISH

Patriots like John Adams, James Otis, and Paul Revere met at taverns in Boston to talk about the problems with England. One of these taverns, called the Green Dragon, was nicknamed "The Headquarters of the Revolution." Although both coffee and tea were originally served at these early restaurants, it was considered un-American to drink English tea during the Revolutionary War. Thanks to history, coffee became America's popular morning drink.

Besides coffee and Honey-Jumble Cookies, what foods were popular during the American Revolution? Can you name popular foods today from different regions of the United States?

snicker-doodles

Nazareth cookies

biscuits

It was George against George during the American Revolutionary War. On the British side King George III and his government didn't like how the colonists kept protesting British laws. On the colonial side George Washington and the patriots had a meeting called the **First Continental Congress** where they decided that Americans should have more say in their own government. If the Georges had been sitting together at dinner, there might have been a food fight.

Then, at the **Second Continental Congress**, something bigger was on the table: independence from Britain. On July 4, 1776, America adopted the **Declaration of Independence**. This document declared that the United States was its own country, separate from Britain. Did that stop the fighting? Oh, no! If anything, it got worse.

The turning point came with the **Battle of Saratoga**. Call it luck, call it smart thinking, but when the patriots won this crucial battle, France agreed to help. With their new allies, Americans won the last major battle of the war, the **Battle of Yorktown**. Victory became official with a different **Treaty of Paris**, signed in 1783. In this agreement, Britain gave up control of America. Huzzah! What celebrating there was for the new United States of America.

I scream, you scream, we all scream for . . . freedom! Around the same time that America was declaring its independence from Britain, the first ice-cream shop opened in New York City. This newfangled dessert was popular, but time-consuming to make by hand. Here are the cold, hard facts: making delicious ice cream—and running a new country—is hard work.

Independence Ice Cream • • • • • • • • • •

Before You Begin

Prep time: 25 minutes
Cooking time: n/a
Total time: 25 minutes

Oven temperature: n/a
Yield: 1 serving
Difficulty: easy

Ingredients

- 2 tablespoons sugar
- 1 cup heavy cream
- ½ teaspoon vanilla
- ½ cup salt (rock salt if you have it, but table salt will also work)
- Ice cubes

Equipment

1 gallon-sized, sturdy zip-locking bag
2 pint-sized, sturdy zip-locking bags
Warm gloves—that ice gets cold!
Spoon
Small serving bowl

METHOD

1 Fill the larger zip-locking bag half full with ice. Pour the salt over the ice.

2 Place the sugar, cream, and vanilla in one of the smaller zip-locking bags. Press out the air before sealing the bag. Place this bag inside the second small, zip-locking bag (double bagging ensures no accidents!).

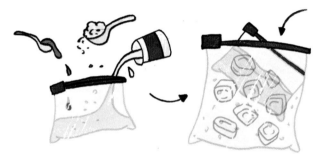

3 Put the sealed cream mixture inside the bag of ice and close this larger bag. Put on the gloves and shake the bag vigorously for 5 minutes (you can share this task with someone else if you want).

4 Put the mixture in the freezer for 4 minutes.

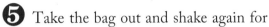

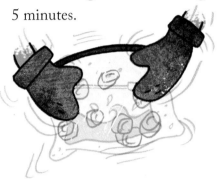

5 Take the bag out and shake again for 5 minutes.

6 The ice cream should be soft now. Repeat steps 4 and 5 for ice cream that is more firm.

7 When ready, remove the ice cream from the bag of ice. Spoon the ice cream into a small bowl and serve immediately.

Independence Ice Cream • • • • • • • • • •

Something to Sink His Teeth Into

The celebrating hadn't gone on long before the delegates got down to organizing a new country. First off they needed a president. Who better for the job than the hero of the war, George Washington? Like everything he did, George sank his teeth right into this new responsibility—at least, he would have. In 1789 when he was inaugurated for his first term as president, George had only one natural tooth left. Instead, he wore a set of false teeth made from hippopotamus ivory and human teeth.

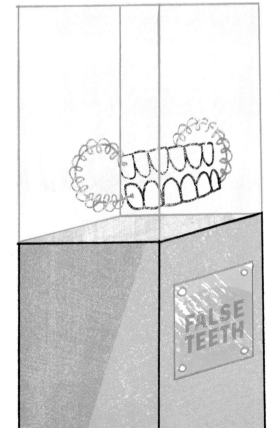

SIDE DISH

During the war George Washington's army was disorganized, untrained, and poorly equipped. Sometimes food was so scarce, soldiers tried eating tree bark or cooking shoe leather. When food was available soldiers often ate salted meat and ash bread (made with flour and water and baked in the ashes of a fire). But watch out—blackened on the outside, this "bread" was often raw in the middle. Unlike the patriots, the British army was well trained and had better equipment and food. At first, the Americans lost battle after battle, and some wondered how long it would be before the British defeated them for good. Not George Washington. He served his soldiers a choice: "To conquer or die."

Even though things seemed bad at first, what advantages did George Washington's army have? Why do you think they were able to defeat the British?

History Review

The Pilgrims at Plymouth, 1620

The Pilgrims were a group of 102 English colonists who came to settle in what is now known as Massachusetts. The Wampanoag people helped them survive. The Pilgrims are credited with holding the first Thanksgiving feast, though the name—and the official holiday—didn't exist until much later.

The Thirteen Original Colonies, 1607–1776

Colonists who came to America experienced many ups and downs as they settled in the thirteen original colonies—later to become states in the new United States of America. They joined (and often clashed with) Native Americans who had been on the continent for thousands of years.

The French and Indian War, 1754–1763

France and England both originally had large colonies in America. They fought over who would control the continent, ignoring the original inhabitants—the Native Americans. France wanted to continue its money-making fur trade, and England wanted a place for English citizens to settle. England eventually won the war, forcing France to give up most of its colonies.

Slaves and the Southern Plantation, 1619–1863

Many Africans, brought against their will to America, were forced to become slaves and work on large town-sized plantations. Their lives were difficult—even so, these early Americans brought with them a rich heritage that helped shape the country of today. In 1865 the 13th Amendment to the United States Constitution made slavery against the law.

The American Revolution, 1775–1783

By the mid-1700s England and the American colonists were quarreling over who had the right to govern the colonies. King George and the English parliament felt it was fair to tax colonists to pay back money England had spent fighting against the French. American patriots were against paying taxes when they had no say in government. The disagreement led to war.

The Declaration of Independence, 1776

On July 4 delegates from the colonies met and signed a document stating that America was an independent country and no longer under British rule. War erupted against Britain with George Washington leading the newly formed continental army. Initially suffering defeat after defeat, Americans finally won and the United States became a new nation.

Glossary

Battle of Quebec (1759): a victory that helped England win the French and Indian War

Battle of Saratoga (1777): a battle won by the patriots in the American Revolution, which led France to agree to help fight against the British

Battle of Yorktown (1781): the last major battle in the American Revolution

Boston Tea Party (1773): when American colonists dumped British-owned tea into the Boston Harbor to protest against the British parliament

Boycott: to protest laws or engage in and express mutual disapproval

Colonist: someone who settles with a body of people in a new land

Declaration of Independence (1776): a document signed by colonial delegates to formally break ties with Britain

First Continental Congress (1774): when delegates from every colony except Georgia met to discuss demands that Britain change the way colonists were governed

Fort Duquesne: an important fort that changed hands several times during the French and Indian War

French and Indian War (1754-1763): the fight between Britain and France for control of North America

Frontier Settlers: colonists who lived away from towns and cities and who had to rely on themselves to provide for everyday necessities

Fur Trade: when Europeans traded tools and weapons to the Native Americans in exchange for valuable animal furs which they sold back in Europe

Hardtack: a hard biscuit made from flour and water that would not spoil easily

Indentured Servants: people who agreed to work for a period of time in exchange for free passage to America

Indigenous people: the Native Americans who were the original inhabitants of North America

Intolerable Acts (1774): harsh laws passed by British Parliament in response to protests by the colonists

Jamestown (1607): the first permanent British colony in America

Mayflower: the ship that took the Pilgrims to America in 1620

Patriots: colonists who wanted American independence and who resisted British laws

Pilgrims: a group of colonists who settled in Plymouth, Massachusetts, in 1620

Plantation: a very large farm, where crops are grown to sell for money

Plymouth (1620): a town in modern-day Massachusetts where the first permanent European settlement was founded

Second Continental Congress (1775): when delegates set up the Continental Army and appointed George Washington as the commander; these same delegates also adopted the Declaration of Independence

Stamp Act (1765): a British tax on printed documents in America

Taxation Without Representation: when colonists claimed that it was not fair for England to demand they pay taxes when colonists had no vote in the British parliament

13th Amendment: an addition to the United States Constitution that made slavery illegal

Thirteen Original Colonies: the first permanent English colonies in America

Treaty of Paris (1763): agreement between Britain and France that officially ended the French and Indian War

Treaty of Paris (1783): another official agreement that declared an end to the American Revolutionary War

Index

N

Native Americans, 4, 7, 11, 13, 17, 19, 23, 29, 42

Nazareth cookies, 34

Netherlands, 13

New Hampshire, 16

New Jersey, 16

New York, 16, 23

New York City, 4, 37

North Carolina, 16

O

Otis, James, 35

P

pain perdu, see lost bread

patriots, 31, 35, 37, 41, 43

Pennsylvania, 16, 34

Pilgrims, 4, 7, 10, 11, 13, 17, 42

Pittsburgh, Pennsylvania, 23

plantations, 24–29, 42

Plymouth, Massachusetts, 7, 17, 42

president, 4, 10, 40

Q

Quebec, Battle of, 22

R

Revere, Paul, 35

Rhode Island, 16

Roosevelt, Franklin D., 10

S

Saratoga, Battle of, 37

Second Continental Congress, 37

slavery, 4, 25, 28–29, 42

slump, *see* grunt

snickerdoodles, 34

South Carolina, 16

Spain, 13

Squanto, 11

Stamp Act, 4, 31

succotash, 6–10

T

taxes, 4, 31, 43

tea, 4, 31, 35

Thanksgiving, 6–11, 42

thirteen original colonies, 4, 13, 16, 42

13th Amendment, 25, 42

Treaty of Paris (1763), 4, 19

Treaty of Paris (1783), 4, 37

turkeys, 7, 11

U

United States Constitution, 25, 42

V

Virginia, 4, 7, 16, 17, 23, 25

W

Wampanoag, 7, 42

Washington, George, 4, 19, 37, 40, 41, 43

Wolfe, General, 22

Y

Yorktown, Battle of, 37

Published by Charlesbridge
85 Main Street
Watertown, MA 02472
(617) 926-0329
www.charlesbridge.com

Library of Congress Cataloging-in-Publication Data
McCallum, Ann, 1965.
    Eat your U.S. history homework : recipes for revolutionary minds/Ann
McCallum ; illustrated by Leeza Hernandez.
        pages cm
    Includes index.
    ISBN 978-1-57091-923-7 (reinforced for library use)
    ISBN 978-1-60734-901-3 (ebook)
    ISBN 978-1-60734-902-0 (ebook pdf)
1. Cooking, American—History—Juvenile literature. 2. United States—History—Colonial period, ca.
1600–1775—Juvenile literature. 3. United States—History—Revolution, 1775–1783—Juvenile literature.
I. Hernandez, Leeza, illustrator. II. Title. III. Title.
TX715.M47426 2015
641.5973—dc23   2014010492

Printed in China
(hc) 10 9 8 7 6 5 4 3 2 1

Illustrations were created using a mixed-media technique combining printmaking, pencil, and digital collage.
Display type and text type set in Blue Century, Adobe Caslon Pro, Humper, and Soupbone
Color separations by Colourscan Print Co Pte Ltd, Singapore
Printed by 1010 Printing International Limited in Huizhou, Guangdong, China
Production supervision by Brian G. Walker
Designed by Martha MacLeod Sikkema